SCOTLAND

Text by Ian Digby

Designed and Produced by

Ted Smart & David Gibbon

Featuring the photography of

Roberto Matassa

COLOUR LIBRARY BOOKS

Scotland and England have been ruled by the same monarchy, and governed by the same parliament, for well over 250 years. The inhabitants of both countries speak the same language and use the same currency. They don't need passports or visas to move from one country to the other and there are no customs posts on the border.

Yet when most Englishmen cross the border into Scotland there is a very definite feeling of entering a foreign country. It is the "Scottishness" of Scotland that sets any first-time visitor back on his heels.

"You see it in the architecture," says Michael Powell in *Alastair MacLean's Scotland* (Deutsch 1972), "in the colossal granite walls of Aberdeen, in the majestic sweep into the heart of Dundee of the road bridge over the Tay, in the fantasies of Scottish baronial, in the purity of the Brothers Adam. You hear it in the speech – direct, literate and colorful – whether broad Lowland or careful Highland. You enjoy it in the abundance of public golf courses; the stupendous high teas; the generous drams of whisky; the electric blankets on the clean beds; the unpretentious goodness of the small things in life."

You see it, too, in the breathtaking sweep of a Highland glen, where the thin winding ribbon of gray road creeping almost apologetically through it seems a concession of nature to man's intrusion. The delicate hues of bracken and heather on either side of the road are broken by a mountain stream that was bubbling when Scotland had its own kings, and a Sassenach Englishman took his life in his hands if he crossed the border.

And you see it in the fickle-tempered islands off the west coast – tranquil and loving one day, angry and violent the next. The people who live there are primarily small farmers and fishermen who exist largely as their forefathers did, living a hard but rich life wedded utterly to the land they work or the sea they fish.

It is the Scots themselves who have given their land this unique sense of identity – no mean achievement for a country of just over five million people.

It has been argued that the Scots have produced more eminent figures per capita than any other people. More than half the total number of American Presidents have Scottish ancestry and many British Prime Ministers have been Scots: Macmillan, Douglas-Home, Gladstone, Ramsay MacDonald. Menzies of Australia and Fraser of New Zealand also had Scottish blood and John Paul Jones, founder of the US Navy, was a Scot. And in many other fields, Scots are internationally acclaimed; Andrew Carnegie, Adam Smith, James Watt, Robert Burns and Sir Walter Scott, to name but a few.

But the irony is that so many Scots achieved their success after leaving their homeland, making their mark on the world in foreign fields.

Alastair MacLean, the best-selling novelist, points out that while the English were battling with the French at Crécy five hundred years ago, Scots were in the neighboring Low Countries doing business and, in some cases, training European armies that in later years would oppose the English.

MacLean, himself an expatriate, believes that his fellow countrymen are "born adventurers. . . . Find a man herding sheep in the furthest reaches of Patagonia and the chances are that he is a Scot. I know of a village in the Italian Dolomites where the most commonly held surnames begin with 'Mac'. . . . The Scots are to be found virtually everywhere." *(Alastair MacLean's Scotland).*

But where did the Scots come from originally? Most historians agree that the first man to stand upright on the rugged terrain of what is now Scotland did so perhaps as long ago as 6,000 BC. Bone and antler fishing spears and other rudimentary implements found mainly along the western part of the country serve as evidence to support this theory.

The Beaker civilization arrived three thousand years later, and lived mainly in henges (of which Stonehenge is one of the most famous). They spread as far north as Orkney, and as far south as Dumfries.

It was not for another 1,500 years or so that the first signs of Scotland's Celtic origins appeared. Around 500 BC the sparse population was roughly divided into two distinct areas. In the north and west, living in "duns" and "brochs", were the people who became known as Picts. To the south and east, mainly in hill forts and camps, lived the Britons who called their land Alba. One of their chief settlements was Din Eidyn (Edinburgh).

The Roman Invasion of Britain isolated the two peoples even further. The Britons capitulated before the Roman legions and over the years of the occupation learned to work with them. The Picts, however, never bowed to Rome and even Hadrian's Wall was not strong enough to keep them from attacking the settlements to the south. As the Roman grip weakened, toward the end of the fourth century, their forces abandoned any hope of suppressing the Picts and, instead, appointed local Briton chiefs to uphold the law, such as it was.

The Irish Connection

But the Picts and the Britons were not the forerunners of the Scots of today. Scotland's heritage, in fact, came from Ireland in the sixth century, with an exodus of Gaels looking for fresh pastures. They landed in Argyll and, when the Irish St. Columba followed a few years later to hoist the flag of Christianity on the British mainland for the first time, the seeds of Scotland's future were planted.

St. Columba established his monastery on the island of Mull and for more than 30 years, until his death in 597, worked tirelessly to spread the Gospel. In doing so, he was instrumental in forging a unity among the people that would later take the shape of a national identity. Before this could materialize, however, a new threat arrived on Scottish shores: Norse invaders, the most frightening war machine of its time. For more than 200 years the land was decimated by Viking raiders and much of St. Columba's work was destroyed. Even the fiercely independent Picts were no match for them. In fact, by the ninth century, the Picts had been all but wiped out, and their territories had gradually fallen under the influence of the Gaelic Kenneth MacAlpine, whose ancestors had come from Ireland.

This period of Scottish history, until the arrival of the Normans from France in the 11th century, is one of its blackest, and represents Scotland's own Dark Ages.

The Norman Invasion directly influenced the development of a Scottish character and entity, for rather than adopt Norman ways, many Northern English fled even further north and established themselves in Lowland Scotland. Their language became known for the first time as Scots. Among those refugees was the Anglo-Saxon Princess Margaret, who later married Malcolm III of Scotland, and devoted much of her life to re-establishing the church in Scotland.

However, Norman influence could not be resisted and a century later, in the 1300s, French was the official language of Court life, of the clergy and of the nobility south of the Celtic lands (largely the Highlands as we know them today), some of which were still partly occupied by the Norsemen.

Scotland could not consider itself a unified country under one king without the removal of the Norse presence. Then Alexander III grasped the dilemma by the horns.

He began to challenge the Norse presence in the Outer Hebrides, and in Orkney and Shetland, angering the Norse King Haakon, who retaliated by ordering an invasion of Scotland. Alexander and his troops met Haakon and defeated him at the Battle of Largs, where a peace treaty was finally signed. Alexander was known as the "peaceable king" and for the next few years Scotland thrived and prospered under his rule.

But peace was shortlived. When Alexander died in 1286, he left no successor, and King Edward I of England saw his chance for a takeover. Using the threat of force, he put his own man, John Balliol, on the Scottish throne. But when Edward called for Scottish support in his campaign against the French, Balliol turned against him. Not only did he refuse the call but, in a bold but foolhardy move, formed an alliance with the French against Edward.

Edward and his army rode into Scotland, bringing death and destruction and ravaging the land. He left behind him a maimed and broken Scotland. He also left with one of the Scot's most treasured national possessions, the Stone of Scone, on which Scottish kings had been crowned. (Sadly enough, the Stone has never been returned to Scotland permanently.)

However, a new hero was to give the Scots hope. Robert the Bruce (more French than Scottish – his name was actually Robert de Brus) gained much popular support and eventually had himself crowned king.

With Edward's death in 1307, Robert began to harass the English forces with guerilla tactics. It was inevitable that there would be an English reaction and it came in 1314, when 20,000 English militiamen massed against a mere 5,000 Scots at a place called Bannockburn.

It became an inspiring victory for the outnumbered Scots, who won against enormous odds, but they were unable to turn it into a real political advantage. It was 14 years before they finally reached agreement with the English, but by then too much had happened to destroy any chance of a cordial Anglo-Scots alliance.

In 1320 an influential group of Scottish nobles and clerics gathered to formulate what became known as the Declaration of Arbroath. It was basically a statement of independence, of the right of the Scots to decide their own destiny, unfettered by London. To give it more impact, they sent a copy to the Pope.

The French Connection

In 1326, building on ties that John Balliol had forged with the French, the "Auld Alliance" between

France and Scotland was formally established. It lasted for centuries, and through it, Scots fought beside Joan of Arc, lined up with the French in the Hundred Years War against the English, and sought refuge in France from English oppression. So close was the relationship that at times it was said: "He that will France win, must with Scotland first begin".

These developments could have only one possible effect: to drive a wedge between the English and the Scots. It has not entirely disappeared even today.

After Robert the Bruce, and the brief reign of the ineffectual David II, Bruce's grandson became king. Known as Robert the Steward, his accession to the throne signaled the revival of a national identity, and the country flourished. It also had another significance: it was the start of the royal line that was to play such an important role in the affairs of Scotland – the Stuarts.

The fifteenth century saw a buoyant Scotland. Trade and commerce expanded, many monasteries were built and three universities – more than existed in England at the time – were established: St Andrews (1412), Glasgow (1451) and Aberdeen (1495).

But fortune did not smile in the same way on the monarchy. After Robert, James I was assassinated in 1437; James II, whose reign began when he was six, was killed accidentally by an exploding cannon, and James III, who came to the throne at the age of nine, was also the victim of assassination.

With James IV, hopes rose once more. Quarrels with England seemed to have been patched up and the future relationship between the two countries assured when James married Margaret Tudor, sister of Henry VIII. But James, an impetuous extrovert, quarreled with Henry (not the easiest of men to deal with) and while his brother-in-law was away fighting the French, James launched an invasion of England. But it was ill conceived and badly prepared. It ended in a major defeat for James at Flodden in 1513.

All that had been gained at Bannockburn, almost exactly two centuries earlier, was lost in a moment of folly and stupidity.

James V succeeded to the throne and cemented Scotland's continuing relationship with France, marrying, first, the daughter of Francis I of France and after her death, Mary of Guise. The latter bore him a child (whom James survived by only a few hours), a daughter who was to become perhaps one of the most tragic figures of history – the future Mary Queen of Scots.

While her mother ruled Scotland as Regent, Mary spent most of her childhood in France, was raised as a Catholic and married the French Dauphin. In 1561, a widow, she returned to Scotland to succeed her mother. But Scotland wasn't ready for Mary. Under the stern, puritanical influence of the Calvinist John Knox, the Scottish parliament had recently denounced Catholicism as extreme and corrupt, and had proclaimed Protestantism as Scotland's faith.

Now they were faced with a Catholic monarch who further angered her subjects by marrying twice more; first to Darnley (murdered in 1567), then to Boswell. Opposition grew too much for her and she fled to London, where Elizabeth regarded her as a threat to the English throne and had her imprisoned in the Tower of London. She was beheaded in Fotheringay Castle.

James VI, the son of her marriage to Darnley, succeeded to the Scottish throne. He had two distinct advantages – he was Protestant and also heir to the English throne, which he inherited on Elizabeth's death in 1603. He became James I of England, and James VI of Scotland.

And so, the stage was finally set for a rapport between the English and the Scots. But it wasn't meant to be. James virtually abandoned Scotland and, when he tried to insist on English-style church services and hymnals in Scottish churches, the Scots, led by the single-minded Knox, resisted.

The struggle resulted in deadlock, and the whole dispute was put aside when the English found their time occupied with a Civil War between the Royalists and Cromwell's Parliamentary forces. The wily Scots saw their chance to further their cause by fighting beside Cromwell and helping him win at Marston Moor. For their support in overthrowing Charles I, Cromwell granted the Scots their Covenants – guarantees of the right to worship as they wished.

But then even Cromwell went too far for the Scots. He beheaded Charles I. The Scots reacted by crowning his son, Charles II, on condition that he also guarantee the Covenants. Charles was forced to flee when Cromwell invaded Scotland. But his return was not long delayed, and, on the Protector's death Charles inherited the English throne, too. This measure was one of the first steps towards the Act of Union which, in 1707, established Scotland and England as one nation, with one parliament, established Protestantism as the national faith and ended forever any real possibility of a Catholic Stuart's accession to the throne.

This didn't stop the Stuarts from making two

determined attempts to overthrow the Act – the Jacobite risings of 1715 and 1745. In 1745, Charles Edward Stuart – Bonnie Prince Charlie – took Perth and Edinburgh, defeated the English at Prestonpans, and with pipes skirling and drums beating, marched as far south as Derby, some 180 miles into England. The English Court was panic stricken and had even made plans to evacuate London when the Scots suddenly retreated.

The Scots were finally beaten at Culloden by the Duke known as ("The Butcher") of Cumberland. The prince escaped the terrible retribution exacted by the English – the Highland Clearances, disarming of the Clans and banning of the tartan – by fleeing to France, where he died 43 years later.

By that time, the Jacobite cause, if not forgotten, had receded far enough into history never again to pose a threat to England or the new, emerging Anglo-Scots relationship. But the unnecessarily cruel and vindictive nature of the English reaction to the uprising was never forgotten, and even now many Scots recall the memory of those days with bitterness.

It may not be an exaggeration to say that the several popular movements for Scottish nationalism since then, culminating in the heady but temporary parliamentary successes of the 1960s, have roots going back to 1745. Nevertheless, since 1745 Scottish history has been completely intertwined with England's.

But what of the land that has seen such a bloody history of its own? '

City Dwellers

Including its 787 islands, Scotland covers about 30,000 square miles – more than one-third of the total mass of Great Britain. The population is widely scattered, but a third of the people live in just four cities: Glasgow (about a million), Edinburgh (half a million), Aberdeen and Dundee (about 200,000 each).

Scotland is traditionally divided into the Highlands and Lowlands, both historically and topographically. The Highlands are the part of the country originally occupied by the Celts. The dividing line between the two sections runs from the northwest corner of Caithness to the southwest border of Scotland, around the Firth of Clyde.

The islands are: The Inner Hebrides (of which Skye is the best known); the Outer Hebrides (including Harris and Lewis); Orkney, Shetland, and the islands of the Firth of Clyde (Arran and others); and of the Firth of Forth (among them Bass Rock). Most of them are inhabited only by sea birds. Less than 150 are home to man.

Glasgow is Scotland's oldest city – there was a settlement at a ford over the River Clyde as far back as AD 500. In the 17th and 18th centuries is was a wealthy market town, and its architecture was widely praised throughout Europe. The Clyde had not been dredged into the major waterway it is today and was still, in the words of Moray MacLaren, ". . . a lowland salmon stream. Around the city by the ford were rich gardens . . . and fruitful farms" (*Shell Guide to Scotland*, Ebury 1965).

Now, of course, it is a major industrial city and seaport. Its size and power are largely the result of a dynamism generated all over Britain during the Victorian era.

The elegant university, a landmark at the top of Gilmorehill, is evidence of this. Built in the 1870's by Sir George Gilbert Scott, it looks dreamily over the western rooftops of the city. The cathedral, which stands on the site of a chapel built by St. Mungo in AD 500, is the only surviving pre-Reformation Gothic structure on the Scottish mainland. The vaulted crypt is one of the best of its kind anywhere in Europe, and the well, in which St. Mungo is said to have performed baptisms, still attracts visitors.

The oldest house in Glasgow stands in Cathedral Square. Provand's Lordship, built in the 1470's, is now a museum. The center of the city is usually accepted to be George Square. It's a gathering place for pigeons, earning for the Square and surrounding streets the nickname, "Dodge City". Along with Catholicism and Protestantism, soccer is a major religion in Glasgow. Hampden Park stadium, with a capacity of nearly 150,000, is one of Europe's largest. There are two dates in the Scottish soccer calendar when all three religions come together, the days when Glasgow Celtic meet Glasgow Rangers. Celtic fans are predominantly Catholic, Rangers mainly Protestant, and although there have been occasional ugly clashes, peace is by and large maintained.

For a long time, a favorite Glasgow pastime has been to take a trip "doon the watter". A Clyde steamer from the heart of the city sails past the great Clydeside shipyards and out into the broad waters of the Firth of Clyde. It's worth the trip to see Ailsa Craig, a 1,000-foot rock rising from the water ten miles off the mainland.

The city is within easy reach of beautiful countryside. Loch Lomond, for instance, the largest enclosed lake in Britain, and nearby Ben Lomond, a mountain which offers some superb views from its

3,200-foot summit, an easy and worthwhile climb. To the northeast lie the beautiful wooded hills of the Trossachs, immortalized by Scott in his famous poem, *The Lady of the Lake,* and also by Nathaniel Hawthorne in his *English Notebooks.*

In the direction of the Grampian Mountains, the Braes of Balquhidder provide some of Britain's best camping country. It was here that the legendary Rob Roy MacGregor led the English a merry chase before the 1715 uprising. He is buried near the ruined church of Kirkton.

The Pass of Killiecrankie is a delightful setting for a walk along the banks of the River Garry as it winds through wooded country. There was a battle between the English and Jacobite forces in 1689 near Killiecrankie. A defeated soldier running from it jumped an unbelievable distance over the river to escape. The spot is now called "Soldier's Leap".

Just up the road is Pitlochry, a major vacation resort where there are excellent facilities for such sports as pony-trekking, riding, skiing and golf. Blair Castle, a few miles away, is the seat of the Duke of Atholl. It is famous as the last castle in Britain to withstand a siege – the one mounted by the Jacobites in 1745. It was rebuilt in 1789 as it stands today, and parts of it are open for viewing.

Travelers through the Grampians are rewarded by superb scenery at places like the Devil's Elbow on the Cairnwell Pass, the highest main road in Britain. This is skiing country and over the past ten years, ski and après-ski facilities have been greatly improved. Glenshee and Aviemore in the Cairngorms offer a huge variety of winter sports facilities such as indoor ski schools, curling rinks, skating, tobogganing and – in summer – pony trekking, rock climbing and sail boarding.

Between the Grampians and the Cairngorms – the highest mountain range in Britain, with several peaks second only to Ben Nevis – lie Braemar and Balmoral on Deeside.

Royal Scotland

Braemar is probably best known today for its celebrated Highland Gatherings, but in 1715 it was where James Edward Stuart first raised the Jacobite banner to herald the Stuart uprising.

The Highland Games have been held at Braemar since 1832, and since Queen Victoria graced them with her presence in 1848 the games have enjoyed royal patronage. The Games consist of piping competitions, tugs-of-war, highland wrestling and dancing, and tossing the caber (which should, according to some experts, be pronounced "cabber"). The word caber means a branch from a tree. In early days it was literally that, with side shoots and leaves removed for the event. There is no standard size, and the point of the event is to throw the caber end-over-end.

Every competitor at the Games must wear a kilt, whether or not he is Scots. Indeed, many competitors these days are not Scots but they still follow the rule and wear a kilt, although not always with precision.

Several other towns – Ballater, Aboyne and Oban among them – also stage Highland Games, but the Braemar event, held every September, is the most prestigious.

The castle at Balmoral is the private residence of the Queen. Prince Albert bought it for Queen Victoria in 1852, paying the princely sum of £31,500 for it. He had it re-modeled with granite quarried right on the 24,000-acre Balmoral Estate. The castle is beautifully situated by the Dee, and although glimpses of it can be caught from the road it is sufficiently secluded to afford the Royal Family its necessary privacy.

The nearest village to the castle is Crathie, and it is to the kirk there that the Royal Family goes to worship when at Balmoral. In the churchyard is a memorial erected by Queen Victoria as a tribute to her faithful ghillie, John Brown. His house is across the Dee and can be seen from the kirk.

The road to Tomintoul – the highest Highland town – winds through the sometimes forbidding Pass of Ballater, extremely narrow in places, and frequently blocked by winter snows. Eventually it wanders into Tomintoul, centered around a village green. The nearby valley of the Avon (pronounced "A'an") is regarded by many as one of Scotland's most beautiful glens.

North of Tomintoul is Speyside, one of the major whisky distilling areas, with Dufftown at its center. Rome was built on seven hills, so the local saying goes, but Dufftown stands on seven stills.

There is more lore and legend connected with whisky than any other Scottish institution. It has its own mystique which canny Scots are careful to perpetuate, with the result that the drink is one of Scotland's major exports. The first record of whisky appears in 1494, but authorities agree it was probably drunk long before that. It is defined as "a spirit obtained by distillation from a mash of cereal grains turned into sugar by the fermentation of malt." There have been many second-rate imitations, but the real thing is in a class by itself. Robbie Burns took it with water, sugar and lemon; Queen Victoria topped her port with it; the purists drink it neat, or with a dash of loch water, but never, never with ice!

A detour toward Aberdeen brings you to the delightful Craigievar Castle. It was built in 1626 and, remarkably, can be seen today almost exactly as it was then. Nothing has been added or changed. In fact, it comes complete with its own ghost, reputedly that of a former owner who was forced at sword point to jump to his death from a window.

The most beautiful approach to Aberdeen is by the coast road. "The one haunting and exasperatingly lovable city in Scotland", as it has been called, stretches elegantly between the Rivers Don and Dee. It is also known as the Granite City, much of it built from local granite mined at Rubislaw, which at 465-feet is the world's deepest quarry. Quarrying has been one of the city's major industries for many years, and Aberdeen granite is found all over the world – in sidewalks, graveyards, office buildings and other places where solid permanence is needed.

But oil is king in Aberdeen today, and you are reminded of its presence under the gray waters of the North Sea by the trappings of the industry visible from virtually every street corner. Plush oil company buildings, fleets of tankers, survey offices and a new crop of leisure centers, bars and restaurants provide oilmen with plenty of ways to spend their money.

Although declining, the fishing industry is still a major employer in Aberdeen, and the daily early morning fish market is a reminder of the city's heritage and is well worth a visit.

Local history is preserved in the Provost Skene's House, the oldest part of which dates from 1545. Within the city the Aulton, or old town, of Aberdeen, belongs for the most part to the University. It has become a stylish mixture of the best of the old with tasteful new student buildings.

From Aberdeen, the search for Scotland continues round the coast through Fraserburgh, with its famous lifeboat station, and Banff, an ancient fishing town, and a stop well worth making at Fochabers. Here, at the end of the 18th century, the fourth Duke of Gordon decided to greatly extend his castle. Trouble was, the village was in the way – so he demolished it.

But he commissioned an entirely new village that today stands as a fine example of Georgian planning and architecture. Ironically, little remains of the castle that brought about such sweeping change.

Elgin, with the remains of a fine 13th century cathedral, lies about ten miles to the west. A few miles inland is Pluscarden Abbey, a monastery that dates back to 1230. For many years its monks have welcomed visitors and delighted in showing them around their early English church.

Butcher's Battlefield

The road runs north through Forres, where Shakespeare set the "blasted heath" of *Macbeth* fame, and on towards Culloden, the burial ground of Jacobite hopes in 1746. A memorial stone mound marks the site where the English forces, under William, Duke of Cumberland, just took 40 minutes to rout the Stuart rebels. During this brief battle, Cumberland undoubtedly committed unnecessary acts of brutality, but he returned to great acclaim in London, where the flower "Sweet William" was named after him. To Scots, however, the flower has always been known as "Stinking Willy".

Skirting Inverness, and running southwest, are the menacing waters of Loch Ness, in some places 750-feet deep. What lurks in those depths? No one knows, but one thing is certain: as long as people want to believe in the existence of a monster the gloomy loch will continue to interest them. If the monster's existence is ever disproved, Loch Ness might fall into comparative obscurity.

Inverness, "the gateway to the Highlands", is also considered the Highland capital, housing many administrative offices for such Highland activities as forestry, deer hunting and small farming.

Urquhart Castle, overlooking the western shore of Loch Ness, has been a ruin for nearly 300 years and much of what now remains dates from 1509. There are two unopened vaults. It is said that one contains treasure, the other plague-infested clothing. But no one knows which is which and, not surprisingly, no one has ever tried to find out.

On through Drumnadrochit and Cannich to Beauly. Not far away is Beaufort Castle, the seat of the Lovat family, once ardent Jacobites. The ruins of the original castle, which was destroyed by Cumberland in one of his purges, can be seen in a terraced garden of the present castle, itself a fine example of Victorian styling.

Between the Firths of Beauly and Cromarty lies the Black Isle; not an island, but a peninsula. It is so-called because of its rich farmland. Snow rarely seems to settle for long on the black soil. In one of its villages, Fortrose, the remains of an ancient cathedral date back to the time of David I.

Dingwall, the county town of Ross and Cromarty, was for many years a Norse town and the name comes from the Norse word "thing", meaning parliament. It is dominated by a tower on the hill overlooking the town, a memorial to General Sir Hector MacDonald. He began life as a cloth maker's assistant in Dingwall, joined the army, was decorated for bravery and rose through the ranks, eventually earning a knighthood. But allegations of homosexuality were made against him (which at the turn of the last century could surely ruin a career in the British Army) and in 1903 he took his own life. To his home town of Dingwall, however, he remains a dashing hero.

Farther north, past Invergordon, where a section of the Royal Navy mutinied in 1931, is the attractive ancient Royal Burgh of Tain. As the birthplace of St. Duthac, it has been a site of pilgrimages for many years. It is also where the wife, sister and daughter of Robert the Bruce were betrayed to their English pursuers. The Collegiate Church there dates back to the 14th century, and there is an interesting prison, housing a curfew bell, presumably used by the English to enforce regulations at the time of the Highland Clearances.

The original structure at Bonar Bridge, over the Dornoch Firth, was designed in 1811 by Thomas Telford, one of England's great engineers, after the Meikle Ferry disaster in which 100 people were drowned.

Dornoch, the county town of Sutherland is, according to Michael Brander, "a medieval town and on top of that a medieval cathedral town...something of a surprise." (*Around the Highlands,* Bles 1967). The cathedral is now the parish church and contains an unusual organ presented to the church in 1907 by the Scottish-American philanthropist, Andrew Carnegie.

Dornoch is perhaps best known for its splendid golf course, which attracts visitors from all over the world. St. Andrews is, of course, the number one Scottish course, and is also the golf capital of the world, regularly holding tournaments that attract the best international players. Its ancient cathedral, castle and university are "musts" for any visit to Scotland. Dornoch also has the distinction of having witnessed the last execution of a witch in Scotland. According to Moray McLaren, "Janet Horn was tarred, feathered and roasted, accused of having turned her daughter into a pony and having her shod by the devil." A stone marks the spot where this unfortunate woman met such a terrible fate.

Gothic Mistake

Farther up the coast lies Golspie, a fishing village and small resort town within easy reach of the beautiful Dunrobin Glen. And a mile to the north is the strangely-designed Dunrobin Castle, seat of the Dukes of Sutherland.

The present building which, says Michael Brander, appears to be "all minarets and turrets, a Gothic mistake", is mainly 19th century. Its contents, rather than the structure itself, are the chief attraction. Part of the castle is open as a museum, housing a collection of mementos gathered by the family through generations, both at home and abroad.

It also contains a fine representation of much of the wildlife found in Scotland, such as polecat, otter, wildcat, pine-marten, badger, fox, stoat and weasel, and most of the exhibition cases bear personal labels written, presumably, by the family member contributing the exhibit.

Wick lies on the coast road to John o' Groats and, like Dingwall, there is evidence of its Norse ancestry. The name comes from the Norse for "bay". The Old Man of Wick, today just a square stone tower, was in its heyday an impregnable castle perched on rocks overlooking the sea, and was probably built by the Norsemen. It's a bustling town with a market and an airport serving the major Scottish cities as well as Orkney to the northeast.

In nearby Sinclair Bay are the ruins of the neighboring castles of Sinclair and Girnigoe. In the latter, the fourth Earl of Caithness, believing his son was plotting against him, imprisoned the young man in the dungeons for seven years, until he died of "famine and vermin".

John o' Groats is called the most northerly point of Britain. However, it is not. That distinction belongs to Dunnett Head, to the west. John o' Groats itself is little more than a sprinkle of white-washed cottages, a hotel, some shops (including the inevitable souvenir stores) and a signpost pointing south that bears the legend "Land's End – 874 miles". This, perhaps more than anything, sums up the size of Britain for the American visitor. The distance from one end of the British Isles to the other is about as far as the distance from Los Angeles to Portland, or from New York to St. Louis.

John o' Groats is named after a Dutchman, one of three brothers who ran the ferry to Orkney in the 16th century. According to the story, when they and their families numbered eight, a disagreement broke out over who was in charge. The only solution was to build an octagonal house with eight doors so that each member of the family could enter by his or her own door and sit at the octagonal table inside without taking precedence over any other. Sadly, the house has long since disappeared.

Between John o' Groats and Dunnett Head, and barely visible from the road, is the Castle of Mey, built in 1567 and now the private retreat of Queen Elizabeth, the Queen Mother.

From Dunnett Head, with its fine sweep of sand, can be seen the Islands of Orkney. There are 67 in all, of which about 20 are inhabited. Mainland is the largest. Its capital, Kirkwall, is 900 years old, with roots in the Norse tradition, and has all the appearance of a Scandinavian town. Stromness, the other main settlement on the island, is much more Scottish. It was a Celtic fishing village until mainland Scots started using it as a port for trade in the 17th century. Hudson Bay Company vessels used to call there regularly too. Now it is content, and quieter, as a small local fishing community.

The second largest Orkney island is Hoy, with a range of spectacular rocky peaks that makes it superb climbing country. The most challenging to the climber is the Old Man of Hoy, a vertical column of basalt rising 450-feet straight up from the western edge of the island. It has been scaled by only the most accomplished of climbers. There is plenty for the historically inclined on Hoy, including an Early Bronze Age tomb known as the Dwarfie Stone. Indeed, nearly all the Orkney Islands are rich in prehistoric artifacts. The Islanders are mainly farmers, and the fishing industry is rare, although visitors find the inland lochs abundant in brown trout.

The Shetland Isles are 60 miles northeast of Orkney. Once you get beyond Unst, the most northerly of them, there is nothing but endless ocean between you and the North Pole.

There are about 100 islands in the Shetlands, some 20 of which are inhabited. Mainland is the largest, with Lerwick, its capital, a maze of narrow streets. It is a cosmopolitan town, often host to foreign fishing crews from Russia and Japan, as well as western Europe. The North Sea oil boom, has brought to Lerwick, as it has to Orkney, the personnel and paraphernalia of oil exploration.

One festival with indelible Viking links takes place in Lerwick each January. This is Up-Helly-Aa, an advance welcome to the arrival of the summer sun following the short days and long darkness of winter. Unlike Orkney, Shetland is mainly a fishing community, but it is also the home of the world famous Shetland ponies, bred on the 25-square-mile island of Fetlar. Shetland wool is also a major industry for the islands.

Part of the British Isles, Shetland, nevertheless, is nearer the Arctic Circle than it is to London. Its remoteness from the British capital was a problem for a Shetlander sending his army draft papers during the last World War. He was asked to enter the name of his nearest railway station. He thought hard for a moment then wrote – quite accurately – "Bergen, Norway". And at that time it was occupied by the Germans!

Back on the mainland, and continuing west along the north shore of Caithness, the stark whiteness of the atomic energy reactor at Dounreay appears on the landscape. Opened in 1960, it was one of Britain's first atomic reactors, a herald of the new nuclear age.

Highland Sport

But just a few miles south, on the moors of Caithness around Altnabreac, lies country that for years has provided the field and stream sports of Scotland, a real slice of the country's heritage: hunting, shooting and fishing, Scottish style.

The Thurso river provides excellent salmon fishing, there are many hill lochs for trout, and on the moors, grouse shooting, deer hunting and falconry.

Grouse are peculiarly Scottish: the Red, found on higher ground, and the Black (the male in fact is ebony and purple with a splash of crimson on his head), near woodland. They are protected for much of the year, but the Glorious Twelfth – of August – heralds the new shooting season, and many of England's leading restaurants go to elaborate lengths to serve the first grouse of the year.

In recent years, Scottish field sports have brought wealthy men from around the world to sample the very special delights of the Scottish moor, once the preserve of the Highlander himself, then of the English aristocracy. There is little to compare with a sparkling day in search of deer, with a knowledgeable local Scot charting the terrain. It is said that the best way to end such a day is to sit down to a meal of venison, cooked by the wife of the head stalker who made the kill.

Across the northern stub of Scotland, heading for the west coast, lies the beautiful, unspoiled Strath Naver, its peace and tranquility belying its stormy history, when small farmers and their families were forcibly evicted from the fertile land in the infamous Highland Clearances. At the southern end of the valley lies Loch Naver in a bowl in the hills. On its northern bank are two rundown, but preserved, 19th century farming townships, Grummore and Grumbeg.

Loch Eriboll lies to the west, a sea loch with a depth of up to 150 feet that makes it a superb natural harbor. About six miles along the coast towards Cape Wrath is the remarkable Smoo Cave. Actually three caves, its largest one is 200 feet long and about 120 high. An 80-foot waterfall plunges into the second cave.

The aptly named Cape Wrath is well known to sailors. Its rugged cliff face rising 400 feet out of the sea, with dangerous reefs below, can be seen from nearly 30 miles. A lighthouse beams out a warning message to seamen.

The road down to the glorious scenery of Suilven leads past the ruins of Ardvreck Castle standing on the shores of Loch Assynt. At nearly 2,400 feet, Suilven is far from the highest mountain in Britain but its strange conical shape rising from the dense Glen Canisp Forest, its renown as a mountaineers' and geologists' paradise, make it one of the most remarkable. Its upper slopes are also abundant in eagle, falcon and buzzard and, lower down, ptarmigan.

To the south lies Ullapool, now a fishing village and tourist center, but once a major port for the Scots emigrating by the thousand to North America at the time of the Clearances.

In some parts around Ullapool live strict sects from within the Free Kirk of Scotland who on Sundays, for instance, remove their tourist bed and breakfast signs, do no washing, and refuse to buy (or sell if they are shopkeepers) milk, food, newspapers, gas and so on. Religion is taken very seriously in these parts: witness the story of a visitor attending morning service in a strict Free Kirk, and joining in lustily with the hymns and responses. The regular congregation, favoring a much more discreet demeanor, grew increasingly annoyed. Finally, one of them complained. "But I'm praising the Lord", the visitor explained. "Sir," said an old churchgoer, "in this church we do not praise anything."

South of Ullapool is the beautiful Corrieshalloch Gorge, a 200-foot gash in the hillside that at certain times of the year has a Mediterranean aura about it. It can be crossed by means of a wire-rope suspension footbridge that swings giddily, but safely, above the ravine, and gives a splendid view of the 275-foot plunge of the Falls of Measach cascading down the head of the gorge.

It is well worth making a detour to the west, and the coastline of Gruinard Bay. Golden sands are fringed by two mountain ranges and there are splendid views over the Minch towards the Isle of Lewis.

Among the most popular attractions on the west coast are the tropical gardens of Inverewe, thriving in the mild, damp climate of Wester Ross, close to the warming Gulf Stream and enjoying more than 60-inches of rain a year. At any time the gardens are lush with vegetation, and imported plants such as Monterey Pines, eucalyptus, and Australian tree ferns grow just as happily as they do in their native soils.

Loch Maree, running south from Gairloch, is one of the most beautiful, the country's first nature reserve, fringed by Ben Eighe, and the majestic Torridon mountain range, and overlooked by the brooding peak of Slioch to the north.

Strome Ferry, on Loch Carron, used to be the departure point for the Isle of Skye and the Hebrides; nowadays the Kyle of Lochalsh has taken over in these parts.

Skye, the most northerly of the Inner Hebrides and the largest of the Western Isles, has its own lore and legend and a very distinct personality of its own. Watching the sun setting over the Outer Hebrides islands of Harris and Lewis from Skye is an unforgettable experience. Just 50 miles long, with the mysterious Cuillin Hills in the south, the Island seems to have a permanent bluish light of its own, except on those very rare, perfectly clear days.

It is mountainous throughout, with the Trotternish range in the north, where you can see the vertical stack or rock called the Old Man of Storr, and the strange rock formation of the Quiraing. Dunvegan Castle, dating from the ninth century, is the seat of the Macleod Clan, and is also a major attraction on the Island. Skye people are as gentle as their soft Highland accents, and with tourism restricted by the limited accommodation available, Skye has remained unspoiled and its hospitality unrivaled.

A few miles to the south lies the Island of Rum, now largely a center for the study of the large Red Deer population and, consequently, not always accessible to the traveler. To the east of Rum lies Eig (pronounced "egg"), a 24-square mile paradise for the botanist and naturalist. A wide range of plant life flourishes there as well as several species of animal life peculiar to the island.

The remaining islands of the larger Inner Hebrides are Raasay, where Johnson and Boswell stopped on their celebrated Highland tour; Rona, which is virtually uninhabited lies between Skye and the mainland; and the islands of Muck, Jora, Islay, Coll, Tiree, Colonsay and Canna.

Anglers' Delights

To the northwest are the Outer Hebrides, consisting of Barra, Eriskay, South and North Uist, Benbecual, Harris and Lewis.

The 1,500 inhabitants of Barra live by farming and fishing and are not reliant on tourists. Three-mile long Eriskay is where Bonnie Prince Charlie first landed from France in 1745, and it retains much lore and legend from that time, with an especially fine heritage of folk songs.

South Uist has a population of about 2,000 (largely farmers), and a tradition of producing the finest pipers. It is only 22 miles long but packed into that length are no less than 190 freshwater lochs – a delight for trout fishermen. It was on South Uist, just a few months after setting foot on Eriskay, that Bonnie Prince Charlie sought refuge after the battle of Culloden and from where he was rescued by Flora MacDonald.

North Uist is much more Norse in character and exclusively Protestant, in contrast to Catholic South Uist. It has many standing stone monuments and, a rare claim in the Hebrides, abundant numbers of salmon and trout. However, the island of Benbecular, probably the flattest of the Outer Hebrides group, is also an angler's dream.

Harris and Lewis are actually connected although they are described as islands. However, they are intrinsically different. Harris is mountainous, rocky and almost exclusively a fishing community where both the English and Gaelic spoken are, to the discerning ear, different from that spoken on Lewis which lies just 30 feet away across a small connecting bridge.

Lewis is larger, flatter and less appealing scenically but Moray McLaren has no doubt that "even among the highly individual Celtic community, the Lewis folk are remarkable ... exhilarating." Lewis is a Gaelic stronghold and Stornaway, its capital, with its bustling, business-like manner, epitomizes the Gaelic character. Weaving, farming and fishing occupy most of the island's population of 20,000. The world-famous Harris tweed comes from both islands, but far more is made on Lewis because a greater percentage of its population is employed in the production of the fabric.

The beauty of the Hebrides, says McLaren, "lies in the spaciousness of sea and sky and land, with their long stretches of sand in which gold and a silvery-white mingle to greet the long Atlantic rollers. In the people of the outer isles still flourishes the essence of Scottish Celtic Gaeldom."

Back on the mainland, and heading south from Strome Ferry, the road leads past the romantically-situated Eilean Donnan Castle, one of the most photographed of all Scottish castles. It stands on a promontory of Loch Duich and overlooks the point where Lochs Alsh and Long join Duich. The structure dates back to the 12th century, but was virtually blasted out of the loch in the 18th century when the English man o' war sailed into Duich and fired broadsides into the castle, forcing the surrender of the Jacobite supporters within; a feat which had previously proved impossible to achieve by land attacks.

At the head of Loch Duich are the peaks known as the Five Sisters of Kintail, each over 3,000-feet high, and just to the north is one of Britain's highest and most picturesque waterfalls – the Falls of Glomach, about 750 feet from top to bottom.

Through the Forest of Glenmoriston, where the Redcoats sought long and in vain for Bonnie Prince Charlie after the battle of Culloden, the road leads down to Fort William, nestled snugly below Britain's highest peak, Ben Nevis. Fort William, established as one of a line of frontier forts to control the Highlands in the 17th century, is now essentially a Victorian town. The old fort was demolished and completely rebuilt to accommodate the arrival of the railroad in 1864.

Ben Nevis rises 4,406-feet, but with its rounded top lacks the impact of lesser peaks. It can be comfortably climbed by the more active tourist on the gentle slopes from Achintee, a round trek that takes about eight hours. But on the other side, the northeast face offers even experienced climbers a real challenge.

The road to Spean Bridge provides spectacular views of Aonach Mor (4,000-feet) and the great corries of Ben Nevis. Spean Bridge was the site of one of the first battles in the 1745 Uprising, and was also a commando-training center during World War II. A dramatic memorial commemorates this fact. Here, too, as at several spots in the Highlands, there is an excellent tartan warehouse.

The tartan was first recorded in the 13th century and is thought originally to have denoted where the wearer lived, rather than clan or name. But the kilt did not catch on until George IV popularized it in the 1820s; before that the tartan was usually worn wrapped around the body in lengths of up to 16-feet, and in earlier days had to be removed before battle.

Glen Roy – a geological curiosity – starts near here.

The Parallel Roads run through this glacial valley, once a lake, on which time and erosion worked to produce this startling phenomenon.

Glenfinnan, at the head of Loch Shiel on the Road to the Isles, is a beautiful spot – romantic even without its Bonnie Prince Charlie associations, commemorated by a monument. It is where the Young Pretender raised his standard to gather the Clans about him for the march on England.

The Road to the Isles ends at Mallaig where the ubiquitous MacBrayne steamers can be taken for many parts of the Hebrides and for Skye. Mallaig is renowned for its kippers – a form of smoked herring fish. Nearby Loch Morar is the deepest inland waterway in Britain and with depths of up to 1,000-feet is surpassed in Europe by only one other lake. Loch Morar, too, is supposed to have a monster lurking below.

Brooding Glen

Cut back inland, around Loch Linnie, and ahead lies Glencoe. "Glencoe is undeniably beautiful," writes Michael Brander, "in a fearsome, rugged way, but I know of no glen in Scotland with a greater atmosphere of gloomy, brooding grandeur." Even, one might add, at the height of the tourist season. Then buses deposit visitors by the hundred, and gypsy heather-sellers ply their wares, and pipers, fresh from Glasgow, play a skirl or two (pipers who probably have never been farther north than Glencoe). Despite all this, the Glen seems able to retain the indelible, gloomy atmosphere created for it by the terrible massacre of 1692, when at least 40 of the Glen inhabitants of the MacDonald Clan were killed by English soldiers under the ignominious command of a Scot – Campbell of Glenorchy.

The clan system – the word derives from the Gaelic meaning family – no longer controls the affairs of the country. At the last count there were some 80 recognized clans (including those with some very un-Scottish names such as Rose and Arbuthnott – but no Scotts or Stewarts).

From Glencoe to Glenorchy the road crosses the forbidding wastes of Rannock Moor, 20 miles of bog and stunted trees that figure prominently in Robert Louis Stevenson's *Kidnapped*.

The Campbell war cry was "cruachan" and the mountain of that name lies beyond Dalmally, guarding the Pass of Brander that leads west to Oban. Ben Cruachan's highest peak soars to 3,689 feet but can be scaled by the reasonably fit. Traditionally, after the Oban Ball, the participants make an early morning climb of Cruachan before a hearty breakfast.

Oban, on the west coast overlooking Mull, is an attractive town of some 3,000 people. Its busy harbor, used by fishing vessels and MacBrayne steamers headed for the Isles, is overlooked by MacCaig's Folly. A circular stadium-like structure, the building was started in the 1890's by a wealthy and eccentric bank manager, MacCaig, who intended it to be a museum. But when he died during the course of its construction his dream died with him.

From Oban, Mull and Iona are within easy reach by steamer. Mull has a great variety of scenery – forest, moorland, hills – and its main town, Tobermory, is a most impressive sight when approached from the sea. Apart from tourism, fishing is now its major industry.

Iona, off the south west of Mull, is famous worldwide. It was to this charming island that St. Columba brought Christianity in AD 563. The Abbey, restored around the turn of the century, holds regular services, and visitors from everywhere come to attend them and to see the work of the Iona Community which was founded in 1938 to maintain the old monastery ruins and the burial place of the Scottish kings. The island itself is a delight, seemingly as untouched and unspoiled as when St. Columba arrived.

The other side of Loch Awe from Oban is Inverary, the county town of Argyll. It is the seat of the chief of the Campbell Clan, the Duke of Argyll. Inverary Castle is one of the chief attractions for the visitor to this delightful town, but it has been ravaged by fire throughout the years. In 1877 there was considerable fire damage and almost 100 years later a more widespread blaze broke out, resulting in the loss of many fine works of art and the closing of the castle to the public.

Going up through Glen Croe to Loch Fyne there used to be a steep climb, and at the top of the pass there is still a stone plaque inscribed "Rest, and be thankful". Many a walker of old was pleased to do so.

Once through the pass, Glasgow is almost within sight, and the traveler is again back in the Lowlands.

Edinburgh, only 30 miles east of Glasgow is, according to its inhabitants, a world apart. It has elegance and style. Princes Street compares with anything Europe has to offer, and the 1,000-year-old castle perched high above the town is a delight to the eye.

As McLaren says: "From Edinburgh's highest point you can see half over southern Scotland and into the

Highland Hills. Everywhere in the streets you may come upon a corner from which you will catch unexpected glimpses of sea or hills or remote countryside."

The city developed at the beginning of the 19th century and until the 1850s simply consisted of the buildings of the Old Town grouped around the Castle on the Rock. St. Margaret's Chapel, built in 1076 and containing so much of Scotland's history, the Canongate Tolbooth, John Knox's House, the Palace of Holyroodhouse, Parliament House (now the Scottish Law Courts), and the Register House are just a few of the places any serious visitor must include in his itinerary.

In the wild Holyrood Park stands Arthur's Seat, a superb 822-foot panoramic vista atop a natural hill. The Edinburgh Tattoo, a fine demonstration at the floodlit Castle of military marching by pipe and drum bands, and the Edinburgh Festival, offering much that is best and new in the arts, are two annual events that bring thousands to this most attractive of cities.

Moving down towards the Border Country, Glen Trool Forest, nearly 200 square miles of national park forest, includes the highest peak in the south of Scotland – The Merrick (2,764-feet) – and the curiosity of a loch within a loch. Loch Enoch surrounds an island which itself has a loch – in this case it is technically a lochan. Robert the Bruce's guerrilla forces at Bannockburn defeated an English contingent in Glen Trool. A memorial at the east end of the Loch records the victory.

Border Country is the land of the River Tweed which, for more than ten miles, actually defines the border between England and Scotland. For that reason it has a special place in Scottish hearts. Sir Walter Scott spent the last 20 years of his life at Abbotsford on its banks. Its waters nourish the rich pastures of the area, its salmon and trout are among the finest, and it feeds the prosperous Border towns of Peebles, Melrose and Kelso – where the tweed fabric is produced.

The border itself runs from near Lamberton on the east coast to Gretna Green, where young couples, under age by English law, used to elope to marry under the more lenient laws of Scotland.

Now discreetly marked by simple road signs, the border nevertheless remains to many Scots the most important one they will ever cross. It can be a highly emotional moment, returning to Scotland, as even many non-Scots have found. Though Scots may leave home, Scotland never really leaves their hearts.

Charles Murray captured the feeling in verse when he wrote:

"Scotland our mither – since first we left your side,
From Quilimane to Capetown, we've wandered far
and wide;
Yet aye from mining camp an' town, from koppie an' karou,
Your sons richt kindly, auld wife, send hame their love to you."

Noted for its beautiful gardens, the ruins of Castle Kennedy with its ivy-clad walls right, is sited in the Lowlands, not far from Stranraer.

Grey Mare's Tail *above*, one of Scotland's highest waterfalls, is sited 8½ miles north-east of Moffat in the spectacular hill country of Annandale.

Lapped by the gentle Gulf Stream, the glorious promontory of the Mull of Galloway *left*, jutting into the Irish Sea, is part of a rich store of beauty in scenic Wigtownshire.

Portpatrick *top right and bottom right*, to the north of the Mull, was once a "Gretna Green" for the Irish, who would sail the 21 miles from Donaghadee in Northern Ireland, and after landing on Saturday, hearing their banns read on Sunday, would be married on Monday. Steamers regularly crossed the channel until 1849 when silting and gales despoiled the harbor.

South of the Royal Burgh of Dumfries on the banks of the River Nith *center right, stands the late 14th century sandstone castle of Caerlaverock* below, *which became a stronghold of the powerful Border family, the Maxwells, during the 15th century.*

In the verdant river valleys of the Border region, where Galashiels, a bustling tweed and woollen town above is set amid the gentle, rolling hills, stand the magnificent, ruined remains of several abbeys, such as Jedburgh below, founded by Prince David, later David I, in 1118 and although in ruins is nevertheless one of Scotland's finest medieval buildings; Melrose bottom left, where the heart of Robert the Bruce is buried beneath the high altar, and Dryburgh top left, the last resting place of Sir Walter Scott, whose body lies buried in St. Mary's Aisle.

It was the beautiful Border country around Abbotsford House center left and right, Scott's home for many years and the scene of his death in 1832, that was a major source of inspiration for the author's romantic novels which were based on Scottish history.

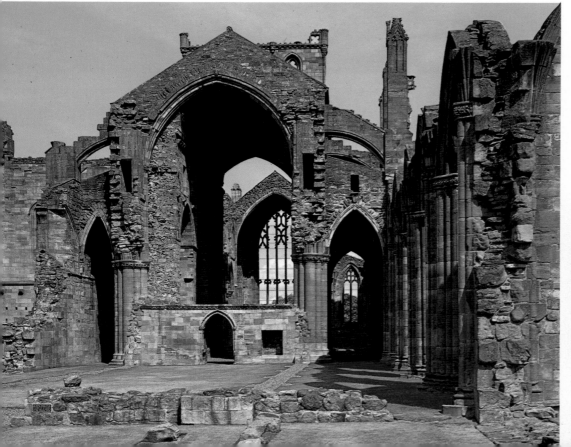

Carrying road and rail traffic from Edinburgh *
the Lowlands, the cantilevered Forth Railway
Bridge, opened in 1890, and Britain's longest
suspension bridge, the Forth Road Bridge,
towering 512 feet above the Firth of Forth, can *
seen left from South Queensferry and above
dramatically silhouetted against a setting sun.

Now lying in ruins, Dunbar Castle, beyond the
crowded harbor right, once sheltered Mary, the
tragic Queen of Scots, before she finally
surrendered to her insurgent nobles in the 16th
century.

Originally started by James IV in 1501, the Pala *
of Holyroodhouse, Edinburgh below, at the foot *
the Canongate, was finally completed almost tu *
hundred years later for Charles II, by the archite *
Sir William Bruce. One of the Queen's Official
Residences, the finely proportioned State
Apartments contain many treasures

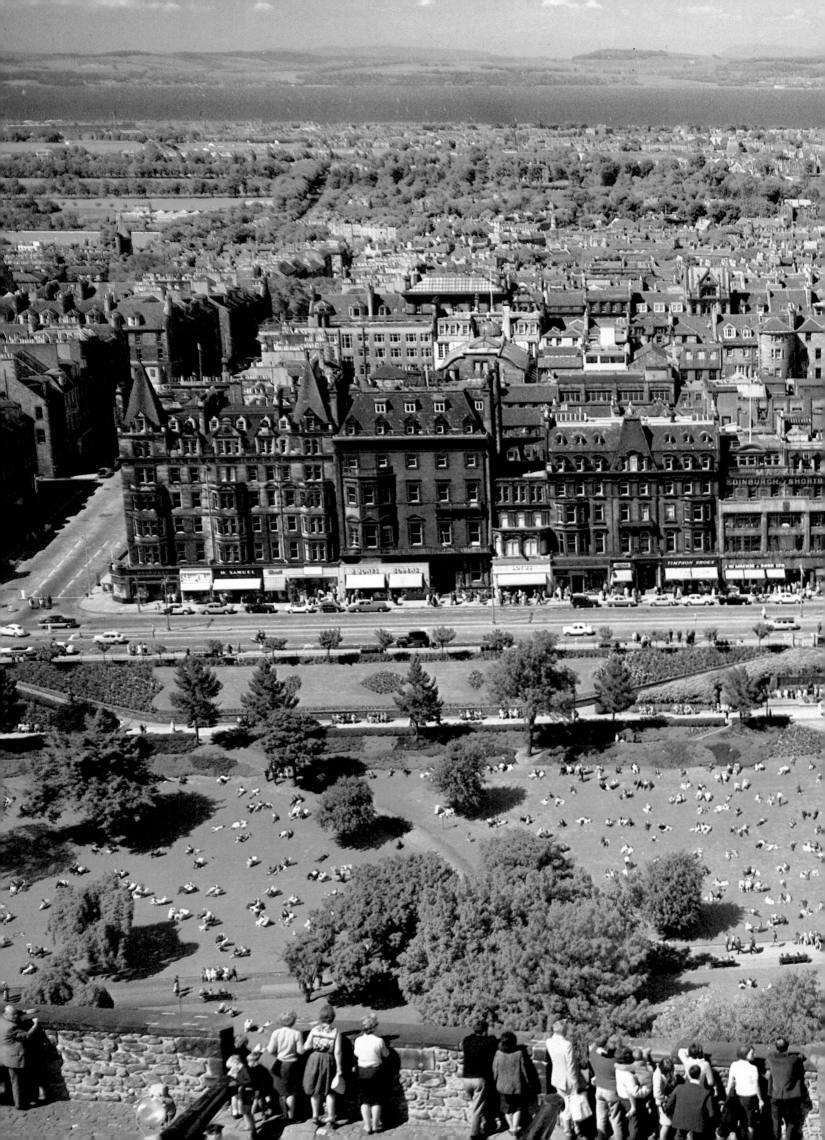

Edinburgh, centered around Castle Rock, on which perch the splendid ruined battlements of the ancient Castle which dominates the blackened city skyline *above left* and seen *above* from the kennel, is Scotland's illustrious capital and the administrative, business and cultural heart of the country. Steeped in history, the city is full of notable buildings and famous streets, such as the Royal Scottish Academy, flanked by the National Gallery of Scotland, shown in the foreground *top right*; John Knox's House in the Royal Mile *center right*, believed to have been the home of the Protestant Reformer during the 15th century and now preserved as a museum, and Princes Street, one of the world's most famous thoroughfares, viewed from the Castle walls *previous page.*

Performed against the floodlit Castle *left*, the Military Tattoo evolved from displays of military drill during the 1948 Edinburgh International Festival and has since become one of the program's most popular items. Traditional pipers at the Royal Scottish Academy Exhibition can be seen *bottom right, and below The Royal Scots Greys Memorial.*

Separating Bute from the mainland as it nestles at the foot of the hilly Cowal peninsula, is the beautiful stretch of water known as the Kyles of Bute, pictured *top left as the P. S. Waverley bottom left* cruises in its calm, sheltered waters. Also in an area of great natural beauty, the Crinan Canal *center left and below connects Loch Fyne and the Firth of Clyde with the Western Isles.*

Ayr, an attractive resort with a fine fishing harbor *above,* and Girvan, a popular trout fishing resort, the harbor of which is shown *right,* are situated along the sheltered Ayrshire coastline, in an area so closely associated with Scotland's national poet, Robert Burns, who drew much of his inspiration from the Ayrshire landscape.

In commemoration of Robert Burns, the Burns Monument above seen from the Brig O'Doon, and the imposing statue above right, are Ayr's memorials to the country's famous bard.

One of the finest Adam houses in Scotland, Culzean Castle left overlooking the Firth of Clyde in Ayrshire, was begun in 1777 for the 10th Earl of Cassillis and incorporates the tower of an earlier Kennedy stronghold.

Standing on land that was once an island, romantic Kilchurn Castle right and below, started by Colin Campbell, founder of the Breadalbane family who erected the keep in 1440, occupies a picturesque position beside upper Loch Awe in Strathclyde.

Glasgow in Clydeside, Scotland's most populous city and an important seaport, has long been noted for its outstanding shipbuilding industry. Among its many fine buildings are the City Chambers on George Square *top right; the Gothic-inspired Art Gallery and Museum* center right, *built in 1902, which stands in Kelvingrove Park, and the extensive University, moved to its Gilmorehill site in 1870 and seen in the background of the Cameronians Memorial* bottom right. *Nightfall softens the harsh industrial outline of the quays and wharves that line the Clyde beyond Kingston Bridge* above, *while* below *can be seen Paisley's impressive Victorian Town Hall, and* left *the famous Cross of Lorraine on Lyle Hill, Greenock, overlooking the Firth of Clyde.*

The west coast of Scotland abounds in idyllic yachting centers: lovely Gourock above, with its picturesque lighthouse below; delightful Largs left, sheltered by surrounding hills that rise to more than 1,700 feet, and tranquil Crinan Harbor top right, a yachtsman's haven on the Sound of Jura. Pictured center right is the popular southern Argyll resort of Dunoon, famous as the home of Burns' sweetheart, Mary Campbell, commemorated by the statue on Castle Hill overlooking the Clyde, and bottom right the triple peaks of the Paps of Jura on this mountainous island, seen from Port Askaig on the Isle of Islay.

Oban, with its picturesque harbor above and
below left and below, *a famous West Highland
resort in Strathclyde, is finely situated on the
shores of a beautiful bay right. McCaig's Folly, the
immense, circular stone structure modeled on the
Colosseum in Rome, which is a vantage point for
impressive views of the town and surrounding
countryside, was built by a local banker whose
intention was to usefully employ the town's
craftsmen during a slump. Although work began
on the project, which was to encompass a
museum and art gallery as well as a memorial to
his family, in 1897, the building was never
completed.*

*Sited south of Oban, Easdale overlooking the
Firth of Lorn above, is set in the lovely Lorn
district which affords magnificent sea-scapes and
island scenery.*

Northern Argyll, Strathclyde, steeped in mountain grandeur above left, where soaring snow-capped peaks rise to heights of more than 3,000 feet and tumbling rivers cascade down wooded glens, is rich in clan and religious history, for this land was the heart of the first Scottish kingdom of Dalriada, whose kings ruled from the hilltop fort of Dunadd.
  Its scenic richness encompasses majestic mountain scenery, seen across the beautiful Glen Orchy below left, and magic seascapes, as well as the great sea lochs, such as breathtaking Loch Etive with its impressive Glen this page, which is bordered on the north-east by the Dalness Forest mountains, and the river which flows through the Glen carrying waters that have risen in the far off Black Corries of Rannoch Moor.

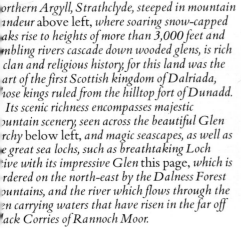

Rebuilt in 1745 beside the blue waters of Loch Fyne, Inveraray Castle *top left and below, seat of the Dukes of Argyll, has, for nearly six centurie been the headquarters of the Clan Campbell.*
Dramatically outlined against a misty sunset, Castle Stalker, Appin, standing on a tiny islet in Loch Laich off Loch Linnhe, is pictured right; *center left the bleak and craggy peaks at Black Mount that stretch between Loch Tulla and Rannoch Moor; bottom left the Kingshouse Hotel nestling beside the River Etive in the shadow of Buchaille Etive Mor, and above the River Beathach in Glen Orchy, in Strathclyde.*

Killin above right, *beside the tumbling River Dochart with its beautiful falls* right and below, *lies at the east end of the mountain-encircled Glen Dochart and Glen Lochay, and is a popular, Central resort offering fishing on Loch Tay, summer touring and winter skiing on the Ben Lawers range. To the west of the town is the picturesque community of* Tyndrum above, *on the River Lochy, while Balquhidder on majestic Loch Voil* left, *in the romantic Trossachs, is best known as the burial place of Robert MacGregor, 'Rob Roy', who died in 1734.*

rling, Central above, *an historic Royal Burgh*
own as the 'Gateway to the Highlands', is
minated by its imposing Castle right *which,*
ched on a 250 foot rock overlooking the
tlefield of Bannockburn, was a royal Scottish
ace until 1603, when James VI became King of
gland.
Delightfully situated in wooded Dollar Glen,
ntral, between the Burn of Sorrow, flowing
ough the steep Windy Pass, and the Burn of
re, ruined Castle Campbell below, *once*
own as Castle Gloume, was burnt by
omwell's troops in the 17th century.
Pictured left *is the meandering River Leny at*
llander, north of Stirling, and above left *tree-*
dded Loch Ard, in the lovely Central area,
th-east of Ben Lomond.

Pittenweem, with its delightful white-washed cottages below, tranquil harbor left, and fishing fleet right, perches, like the picturesque fishing village of Crail overleaf, on the rocky coast of East Neuk in the Kingdom of Fife – home of Scotland's kings from Malcolm III until the Union of the Crowns. Cut off from the rest of the Central Lowlands until the mid-1960's, when the two great road bridges over the Forth and the Tay ended Fife's isolation, the area is now rapidly developing as a popular tourist area.

Amid the charming cobbled streets of Culross, lined with 16th and 17th century red-tiled houses, stand the 'Study' and Cross above, excellently maintained by the National Trust for Scotland.

Fife is possibly most famous as the home of golf – believed to have been played here in the 15th century. Founded in 1754, The Royal and Ancient Golf Club of St. Andrews, with its famed Road Hole, the seventeenth, on the Old Course which is shown right, is today the foremost in the world.

Pictured above and below *is the university city of St. Andrews, the now-ruined cathedral of which was founded in 1161; left Anstrutter, beneath a brilliant rainbow arch, and above left a further charming view of Pittenweem Harbor.*

Standing between the meadows of the North and South Inch at the head of the River Tay estuary, the 'Fair City' of Perth in Tayside *above and right was Scotland's capital for a century until 1437. South-west of the city lie the world-famous Gleneagles golf courses* center left *which spread like a verdant carpet over the moorland between Strathallan and Strathearn, where picturesque Crieff* top left *nestles on the hillside above Strathearn. Drummond Castle, situated two mile south of Crieff, is shown* bottom left, *and* below *idyllic Port of Menteith on beautiful Lake Menteith in the Trossachs.*

Tayside's magnificent wooded scenery and turquoise lochs have long kindled the imagination of visitors to this scenic area: admiring the beautiful view of Loch Tay from the stone bridge over the River Tay at Kenmore top left, Burns was so impressed that he set it to verse, and Queen Victoria, gazing across Loch Tummel bottom left from the north bank, now aptly named Queen's View, was enchanted by the westward vista of snow-capped Schiehallion rising to a height of 3,547 feet and seen below right beyond tranquil Loch Rannoch. East of Loch Rannoch lies the new and dazzling Loch Faskally above right, created by a 54 foot-high dam at Pitlochry, which is part of the area's extensive hydro-electric developments.

From the Hermitage Bridge close by the small cathedral town of Dunkeld, in the wooded Tay valley, can be seen the majestic, cascading Falls of Bran center left, while nodding daffodils bring springtime to the pretty market-town of Aberfeldy above.

Standing at the meeting-place of several glens, not far from Blair Atholl, lovely Blair Castle below, built by the Duke of Atholl in 1269, is set amid Tayside's splendid highland scenery.

Picturesquely dotting the Grampian landscape
are a wealth of beautiful castles, including the
turreted Midmar, of late 16th or early 17th century
baronial-style architecture left; fascinating
Braemar, perched on a bluff overlooking the Dee
below, and one of the country's finest ecclesiastical
buildings, dating from the 13th century, that of
ruined Elgin Cathedral right.

Lying one mile north-east of Cruden Bay is the
Bullers of Buchan above, a vast 200 ft-deep
chasm in the craggy cliffs that jut out into the
North Sea.

Aberdeen these pages, *Scotland's largest fishing port and recently of major importance as the North Sea oil capital, is also a noted university and cathedral center, lying on the estuaries of the Rivers Dee and Don. In addition to being Northern Scotland's leading commercial center, the Royal Burgh also attracts many summer visitors as one of the country's largest coastal resorts.*

Aberdeen, captured as the sun's last rays throw deepening shadows over the city skyline, is pictured top left and below; center left the little fishing village of Crovie, nestling beneath the lofty red cliffs in Gamrie Bay; bottom left Macduff, an important herring-fishing town in Banff Bay; above picturesque Findochty, lying on a rocky stretch of coast between Long Head and Craig Head, and right the all-year-round Highland resort of Aviemore, set near the foot of the historic rock of Craigellachie.

Fine views of the snow-tipped Cairngorms can be seen from the popular Speyside resort of Newtonmore above right; below beautiful Loch Morlich at Aviemore burnished by a setting sun, and right the autumnal tints at Loch Moy, eclipsed by the advent of winter above.

Stories of an awesome monster said to lurk in the depths of Loch Ness left, overlooked by the impressive ruins of Urquhart Castle overleaf, date back at least to the 7th century, but despite hundreds of purported sightings the mystery continues . . .

Misty sunsets in frosted winter landscapes, over wooded Loch Laggan above and right, and mysterious Loch Ness left, enhance the majestic Highland scenery.

A magnificent piece of 19th century engineering, the Caledonian Canal below, begun by Thomas Telford in 1803 and opened forty-four years later, once provided a safe, alternative passage to the stormy route round Cape Wrath. Made obsolete by the coming of large steamships, today this unique canal is mainly used by pleasure craft and fishing boats.

Dredged by a thick coating of gleaming snow, Ben Nevis, at 4,406 feet Britain's highest mountain, seen from the Caledonian Canal *top left*, and Banavie *right*, dominates Fort William which nestles at its base *above*, and the Highland district of Lochaber from the south-west end of Glen More.

At Banavie a chain of eight locks on the Caledonian Canal, pictured *bottom left* as ice-floes still the rushing water, is popularly known as 'Neptune's Staircase'.

Backed by lofty hills, the Highland village of Tulloch *center left* stands on the River Spean in Glen Laggan. Sited close to Spean Bridge, Scott Sutherland's impressive memorial, dramatically silhouetted at sunset *below*, commemorates the commandos of the second world war.

Lying in the Great Glen of the Highlands is tranquil Loch Unagin *left* and Loch Oich *above,* the highest of the chain of lochs which are linked together by the Caledonian Canal. Loch Linnhe, at the extreme west end of the Great Glen (Glen More), is seen at its best from the steamers, such as the 'King George V' *above right, as they sail from Fort William to Oban during the summer months.*

Burgeoning spring, with its dancing daffodils and green-tipped shoots, brings color to the Highlands *right,* while the granite mass of 500 million-years-old Ben Nevis soars into a summer sky beyond verdant Glen Roy *below.*

The skirl of the bagpipes *below* resounds through the magnificent, savage mountains which overhang celebrated Glencoe *right*. Often called the Glen of Weeping, it was the scene of a terrible massacre in 1692 when a troop of soldiers, led by Robert Campbell of Glen Lyon, slaughtered MacIan and more than forty Macdonalds – their hospitable hosts for twelve days – since the Macdonalds had refused to yield their Jacobite cause. In memory of the slain chief, the monument *bottom left* stands near the entrance to the glen.

Warm tints of summer on Loch Leven, near Ballachulish *top left*, are transformed by a crisp, white blanket of snow *center left*, while a glowing sunset envelops the majestic cliff scenery of the Isle of Mull *above*.

Running through magnificent mountain scenery from Rannoch Moor to Loch Leven in old Inverness, Glencoe, with its brooding, precipitous elevations, such as the Three Sisters – Beinn Fhada, Gearr Aonach and Aonach Dubh – at the head of Glencoe *above left, and the majestic twin Buchaille Etive peaks, overshadowing the picturesque climber's hut* center right, *which are separated by the Lairig Gartain Pass and face the lovely Glen Etive, is one of Scotland's wildest and most famous glens. The Pap of Glencoe, rising beyond densely forested slopes* above *and seen across Loch Leven and Glencoe Village* bottom right, *is sited at the entrance to the glen and is a prominent feature of the view from Ballachulish, while winding through the awe-inspiring Pass* below left and top right, *is the cascading Glencoe River* below and overleaf.

Inhabited by red deer, golden eagles, ptarmigan and wildcats, this fascinating, scenic glen offers some of the best mountaineering terrain in Scotland, as well as superb routes for hill-walking.

A large herring-port on the rocky shores of North Morar, Mallaig, with its delightful harbor *left and below, is the western end of the composer's "Road to the Isles" and a popular starting-point for touring the legendary Isle of Skye.*

Overlooking Loch Shiel in a dazzling mountain setting, the monument at Glenfinnan *right and overleaf* stands regally on the spot where Bonnie Prince Charlie raised his father's standard on 19th August 1745, at the start of his attempt to recover the lost Stuart crown. West of the monument, beautiful Loch Eilt *above* is set in the wild Highland scenery of this heavily indented Atlantic edge of Scotland, towards the Sound of Arisaig.

*Curving through the overhanging mountains,
Glenfinnan Viaduct is pictured above, bordered
by the jewel-like waters of Loch Shiel, and* right
*as winter's heavy fall of snow blots out the summer
greenery, while autumn mists tint tranquil Loch
Eil center left and seen* below *against the
towering bulk of Ben Nevis.*

*East of the white-sand-fringed bay at Morar
top left stretches beautiful Loch Morar, Britain's
deepest inland water at 180-fathoms and
reputedly inhabited by a monster which is said to
appear whenever a death is imminent in the Clan
MacDonald.*

*Built by Sir John Comyn, one-time regent of
Scotland, the ruined 13th century Inverlochy
Castle bottom left is sited two miles north-east of
Fort William, overlooking the mouth of the River
Lochy.*

The magnificent Highland scenery of Glen Shiel, touched by winter's crispness top left, inspired Dr. Johnson to write his now-famous 'Journey to the Western Isles' when, in 1773, accompanied by Boswell, he rode on horseback through the glen. Overlooking Loch Duich, at the east end of the glen, the celebrated Five Sisters of Kintail center left rise majestically from the roadside, while to th west stands the contoured outline of the precipitou Saddle, its 3,317 feet blanketed by thick drifts of snow above.

Breathtaking views of Beinn Eighe and Liathach are pictured bottom left beyond the island-strewn Loch Carron, flanked to the north-west by a thickly-wooded national nature reserve.

Dramatically situated on an island at the meeting point of Lochs Duich, Long and Alsh, the Jacobite stronghold of Eilean Donnan Castle above and below right, below and overleaf, built by Alexander II of Scotland in 1220, was held by Jacobite sympathizers during the early 18th century rebellion when it was bombarded by the English warship, the 'Worcester'. In 1932, however, the MacRae family reconstructed the ruin and today this imposing edifice houses a museum and clan war memorial.

Named for an early King of Norway, Kyleakin *above and top right, on the Isle of Skye,* overlooks the narrow strait of Kyle Akin through *which the Norwegian king sailed on his journey to Largs. To the east of the village stands ruined Castle Moil* bottom right, *affording magnificent views of Loch Alsh, and for centuries a stronghold of the Mackinnons of Strath. Beyond Tarskavaig* left, *the serrated Cuillin Hills* center right *are shrouded in a misty sky, while* below *a solitary yacht basks in the autumnal sunshine of Loch Ainort, in this picturesque island, steeped in 4,000 years of myth and history.*

Ranged along the breathtaking sheltered inlet of
Loch Carron, the charming fishing and craft
community of Plockton top, center and bottom
left and above, flanked to the north by the
Applecross and Torridon mountains, which appea
to rise like specters from the turquoise waters of
Loch Torridon below, forms part of the
Balmacara estate in this wild and rugged
Highland region. Linked to Torridon by a road at
the head of the loch affording superb views of the
red Torridonian sandstone peaks, is Shieldaig
right, picturesquely situated on Loch Shieldaig, an
inlet of majestic Loch Torridon.

Throughout the Highland region superb coastal scenery and rugged mountain splendor combine to make the area a tourist paradise. Backed by the craggy mountains of Reay Forest, Kinlochbervie, on Loch Inchard, can be seen top left; center left the small coastal resort of Lochinver, in the Assynt district, at the stony head of Loch Inver; bottom left the noted east coast leisure center of Wick, offering a host of fine facilities, and right the leading sea-angling center of Ullapool, near the mouth of Loch Broom. Pictured above are the striking rock formations of Muckle and Little Stacks at Duncansby Head, off the northern mainland coast, and below imposing Dun beath Castle on its lofty promontory, one mile south of Dunbeath.

Beyond John o' Groats overleaf near the extreme
north-east tip of the Scottish mainland, lie the
stepping-stone islands of the Shetlands and the
Orkneys. Of the 100 Shetland islands less than
20 are inhabited, with Lerwick, the pretty small
boat harbor of which is shown above right, the
capital, situated on Mainland—the largest island.
On the east coast of Yell, separated from
Mainland by the Yell Sound, is the port of Mid
Yell left. Skara Brae above, a remarkable
neolithic village settlement, stands on the largest
Orkney island of Mainland, north of Stromness
with its fine harbor right, while the island's
capital, Kirkwall, clusters around the red and
yellow sandstone St. Magnus' Cathedral below.

First published in Great Britain by Colour Library Books Ltd.
CLB 1289.
This edition published 1985.
© 1985 Illustrations and text: Colour Library Books Ltd.,
   Guildford, Surrey, England.
Display and text filmsetting by Focus Photoset, London, England.
Produced by AGSA in Barcelona, Spain.
Colour separations by Fercrom, Barcelona, Spain.
Printed and bound in Barcelona, Spain by Rieusset and Gráficas Estella.
ISBN 0 7112 0041 6